To an Unknown Shore

Selected Previous Publications by Theodore Enslin

The Work Proposed (1958)
This Do (1966)
New Sharon's Prospect & Journals (1966)
Characters in Certain Places (1967)
2/30–6/31. Poems, 1967 (1968)
Forms 1-4 & Coda (1970–1974)
The Country of Our Consciousness (1971)
Sitio (1973)
In the Keeper's House (1973)
With Light Reflected: Poems 1970-1972 (1973)
Fever Poems (1974)
Mahler (1975)
The Median Flow: Poems 1943-1973 (1975)
Some Pastorals: A New Year's Cycle for Jake (1975)
Carmina (1976)
Ascensions (1977)
Ranger CXXII & CXXVIII (1977)
Concentrations (1977)
Tailings (1978)
May Fault (1979)
2 plus 12 (1979)
Star Anise (1980)
Madrigal (ca. 1980)
In Duo Concertante (1981)
Markings (1981)
September's Bonfire (1981)
"F. P." (1982)
Meditations on Varied Grounds (1982)
Grey Days (1984)
The Weather Within (1985)
Music for Several Occasions (1985)
The Waking of the Eye (1986)
Six Pavannes (1987)
Love and Science (1990)
Gamma Ut (1992)
Mad Songs (1995)
Thumbprint on Landscape (1997)
Sequentiae (1999)
Then and Now: Selected Poems, 1943-93 (1999)
In Tandem (2001)
Nine (2004)
One Summer's Daydream (2006)
The Place Where I Am Standing (1964)
To Come, To Have Become: Poems 1961-66
The Four Temperaments (1966)
The Diabelli Variations & Other Poems (1967)
Agreement and Back: Sequences (1969)
Views 1-7 (1970)
Etudes (1972)
The Swamp Fox (1973)
Views (1973)
The Mornings (1974)
Of East Dennis: The Highlands in Sorrow
Ländler (1975)
Synthesis 1-24 (1975)
The July Book (1976)
Papers (1976)
The Further Regions (1977)
Circles (1977)
Ranger (2 vols. 1978; 2nd edn. 1980)
16 Blossoms in February (1978)
Opus 31, no. 3 (1979)
The Flare of Beginning Is in November (1980)
Two Geese: Two Poems (1980)
The Fifth Direction (1980)
Axes 52 (1981)
Processionals (1981)
Fragments Epigrammata (1981)
To Come Home (To) 1976–1979 (1982)
A Man in Stir (1983)
Songs w/out Notes (1984)
For Mr. Walters: Master Mechanic (1985)
The Path Between (1986)
Case Book (1987)
From Near the Great Pine (1989)
Little Wandering Flake of Snow (1991)
Music in the Key of C, Part 5 (1995)
Propositions for John Taggart (1996)
Conversations (1998)
Re-Sounding: Selected Later Poems (1999)
Six Music Lessons (2000)
A Folder for L.N. (2003)
One Day and How It Was (2005)
I, Benjamin (2010)

Theodore Enslin

To an Unknown Shore

Poems 2009-2010

Shearsman Books
in association with Skysill Press

First published in the United Kingdom in 2017 by
Shearsman Books
50 Westons Hill Drive
Emersons Green
BRISTOL
BS16 7DF

Shearsman Books Ltd Registered Office
30–31 St. James Place, Mangotsfield, Bristol BS16 9JB
(this address not for correspondence)

www.shearsman.com

ISBN 978-1-84861-555-7

This volume is published in association with Skysill Press, Nottingham.

Contents

for Alison
and
Michael, Whit, and the two Johns

Some things newfound   already known

Night Study

Moon sickle above under
brush where it always was
crumble in flames of echo
where it always was in
clouds   of a last reflection
sound   only mouse footfall
silence   dark depth to plumb
onshore of little breeze
no wavelength   light to touch
as phosphorous fish scale
light poured into shadow
no live thing remaining
spindrift   footstep in it
sickle moon   it dies away.

It is what we have dreamed
what we have not   or
what we think of it
changing shape we move
more easily than we do
on waking   shape changed
It is a logic to turn younger
or shape changing perhaps
to become a cat or a fish.

It is more real than the dream
or an actual breath.

Part of the land
a dry void
not fallen to the sea
yet
as yet becomes all that
we can say or see
not a dooryard fenced
from the many others
or resembles
only *this* part of *that* land
and the sea will claim it.

There is a precision that remains
though fog will attempt to deny it
the rocks which seem unseated
are upon the ground and into it
as far as gravity will take them
there is precision in the air above
though it seems less stable
it cannot be   only the voices that echo
against what is solid   they are not precise.

The sea in evidence
that there is more than land
some will not believe it
clinging to old furrows
that change but more slowly
the sea which is evident
in its flux which is constant
as they will see if they dare try
and the contrasts do come
across the waves in length
and an austere   breadth
evident in those changes
as all of this comes from water
and the stones continue
in their weeping.

The Scare

I had not thought to be afraid
the fragments of the day seemed normal
not to be avoided   so I walked on
a sudden burst   wing or footfall
changed what I felt by feather or hoof
anxious at first giving way to terror
suddenly gone   as if only a passing cloud
that the sun relinquished
soon after   and I passed on.

The past cannot soar above us
except in smoke from
where it has been used
a smoke lighter than the air
surrounding it.

I mean to be serious about this
but cannot suppress a laughter
which is not a titter
the past which smiles and frowns
far from   yet with us.

There is the sound of a hammer hammering somewhere
close but not close enough to where it might be
where or why it is hammering   sound not scattered
close enough to hear it   but no other reason for it
Perhaps each stroke is accurate or not precise enough
telling so little   stroke on stroke   to fit the nails.

Grooved for the ass
an old deck chair
rusty   much of the paint
gone from that groove.

To seek out is not to find
nor should it be thought
a sure way   merely
the curious light from eyes
one attempt more which equals journey.

As if there were time enough to notice
that stones will polish in the wind
or that's an accident of speech
where happening has nothing to do
with thought   the laggard as it always was
but still the rock face brightens
while sand will sink away from it.

A Bond

If I have spoken to a tree
say an oak   I did not expect it
to answer me   yet some trees have
left me with the surprise of a strange happening
which   while it may be an answer
took me elsewhere   out of myself   a reckoning
that changed at least the ground on which
we stood   I poised   that tree still rooted
yet different   the difference reaching
beyond our understanding no doubt
something other than a recognition.

So this one dropped   and I won't find it
not to explain this   trying to look for other leaves
as if from 'leafing through'   I did look   but why?
hard enough to look down   particularly in the dark.

Shock

Not to recognize whatever it was
trembled or trembling against the vibration
glass or the frame around it   window
to pick up below the sound but not
the sound itself   move dexter or sinister
all hands on   not to bear recognizance
as of precision before the fall   a swaying
precarious   preceding a fall to remember
this much more with it   no way not to
in description find it in tremor sounding
thus the tree falls.

Age   eventually   turns its tricks
what we have not seen   or felt   we do
that forehead   smooth   and suddenly the lines
which lay there are imprinted
left as footsteps leave their marks
and sand will shift to cover them.

How Many Times

The moon's come in by no one's bidding
or what we see and call the moon
reflected light is scarcely light
although it lights and lightens us
it catches on whatever's here
implied   reminds us to make an ordering
moves on   we later say the moon's gone out.

What is wild in our own day
is not the wild that's past
there is a different savor
some of it not pleasant
perhaps it never was
but it differs now
does not depend on distances
as it once did   now
the wildness is within us
trying to get out
one day it may   but without us.

A Greek Trip

Rough breathing on the way upstairs
hard without help   hard   hard   hard
smooths out at the landing but returns
when going down   'oh world
oh life oh time'   a pleasant jingle
darkens   'on whose last steps I climb'
hard   beyond the easy stretches
rough   hard   rough the breathing.

Gardener Pass By

No need to covet
sight and scent are
quite enough
if you have seen it
in its place that's
because it is not for you
it might be well to think it
not what you call your own.
Pass by I say   PASS BY!

It is too easy to say it
to be alone is not to be lost
or it may be if alone is lonely
There is a difference   deflected
many of us have known this
to be alone one thing
to be lost another
                                        depending.

The known so close to the unknown
that they often interlace and lock
the branches alive on separate trees
enough to see this in the air
the sinew of the bark
even when leaves drop.

A Common Experience

There is a simulacrum
Best that it is not forgotten
by thought or the theft
of fair copies   or others
thought important
they spring from what is common
to all of us   the outlines
are not strange to any
though we may strive to
to make them new.

Of Certainties   No Politics

The eye   stripped naked
sees pitiless what there is to see
the eye is vulnerable   it loses
focus and goes dim   as nothing more to say
less and less to see.

One Night On Waking

So still   So quiet
if a pin should drop
somewhere in the universe
there might be reverberation
louder than a thunderclap.
So quiet   so S T I L L.

To put life or fire into a word?
No   those were always there
but the use of many words
will often bring what was there
incipient   to ruin take care
how you hold what has a heat that
may crumble into ashes.

Of Vision

As she said “Glad I didn’t crush it”
thinking of a shadow   but how could she?
passing through what was not a solid presence
illuminating the other presence of what was fragile
and more to be avoided   with sharp edges
no   she walked in what preceded darkness
avoiding purpose of a leaf or twig
not what she meant   what she said still sounds
“Glad I didn’t crush it”
re   verberating.

What is heard has passed us by
music is in aftermath   not its stroke
to remember is in ordering
split and then returned to say
to hear before the echo.

A ring of changes
bells and circles
something round around us
changes in a measure
a breath so changed
rings these changes
becomes the circled ring.

Thank you as polite dismissal
is nothing more   and nothing more to say
what's more?
To ask a favor   please
please   please   it all amounts to
thank you   such a silence.

There is a wind that strikes
the many directions some not given us
'go west' is one way to try
to make it right reckoning
but it is not enough
there are more ways to tell us where to go
their hells are bonfires   only speech.

One drop however it might fall
from whence to where a
matter of its falling not in question
here to there might be an asking
set askew   from which of many clouds?
not what's to set in place
its quality of wet almost forgotten
it remains apart   how many others
only this remark upon one drop.

There is nothing that will defeat the light
not what we intersperse against the darkness
such lights are not the same   nor a chance
to read these words against a flicker
lit   fire   light.

Life Long

C.C. – W.C.W.

‘I played no games’   and that was game enough
it made for other gamesmanship
As one man put it many times
‘Ain’t it enough?   I did the work.’

Virelai Old Style New Made

Well, once upon a time I stole a kiss
but that was no time to measure when
new light will brighten as it warms
these things become as one that kiss
that I am now as ever was.

Censors Resign!

Say whatever it is you want to say
there is little harm in any of it
all said before to those we want to protect
from what?   Say on and do not blur rough edges
sound above the real sound   read on what's there
those of you who can and without dependence
on such things as those you call mixed media
let no one look across your shoulder
nor stuff with wax your many senses
go on and say   we need to hear.

There are flowers of sadness in that year
when seasons crowd each other   come too early
when the blooms come too early for this place
and winter seems far off   but is not
every day one step   that much clear
grey hairs upon a girl still young.

Michaelmas Daisies

—how they bloom and die
as all the rest—
given their own time
best of it   not the known
no place to settle
only this pot tipped
on its side
damned late in the fall.

There is another cloud   another and
another   in terms of acceptance
some may think it in that way
not in legend   a ritual another and
another   another and another
some die away   others trailing.

The air as
pane of glass
through which to
see what is there
to see seeing
only as breath
taken   a surprise
to see through
window glass
is only air

There is always something to deter
what 'it' seems to be
Eyes that open unaccustomed to the light
catch some things as they are not
or not in ways seen usual
what we *think* is usual
would be to another waking
other eyes that open other ways to see.

Bring
down
the
beat
from
where
you
thought
you
heard
it
Not
its
music

Hermit Thrush

The singing's always new
the melody is old   or not
usually it is where
nothing new to sing or say
or sing when saying's not enough
or gives new voice(s)
Listen to the solitary   thrush
his heritage is full of sound
much of it what's not known.

Cast the deckloads if you can
the ship will not right itself
in such a storm under heavy burdens
these are hard times at sea
if the voyage lasts beyond a crossing
bridges will not do
return home light you mariners
some ships will return
if not this one you steer near port.

Heroes live best unsung
metals are false that shine
first cut or minted
air that breathes around them
heroes or the common color
let the winds decide
that first or final breath.

Shadow of the thing itself
becomes it   of another color
thing not touched and not to be
not in copy   but what is there
in shape its constancy
the touch the shapes they have now
substance other than a symbol
these leaves reflected on whatever
in this light remains the true beginning.

Points of Departure

So saying   what was
said:
        The arrow may be used again
the bullet is less likely
both agree at trajectory
the life beyond can differ.
(So to say).

As if to cross the land
to come and find
the sea again
the land created by retreat
in flux or tide
the sea returns
there is no permanence
the rock will smile
beyond the sight
of those who claim it
no claim is valid
unless the seas lay claim
and then relinquish
what belongs to them
what will again
until there is no wet or dry
blood seems a property
of ultimate reclaiming
as if to cross
the coming tides.

A Tentative Tribute to C.C.

From such a language
as no words can say
without the wording
it leaves me breathless.

A Scope of Remembrance

—if it does cohere
it is the coherence of a gravity
in pull of attraction   one that maintains
impingement at the lowest level
an impasse of foundation
we see only the surface that catches light
and that reflection which coheres
with another source   the immensity
that joins in myriads of touch
awash and restless as the seas   coherences.

Overheard

Sibilant
            as a voice coherent to another
one not heard distinctly
                        not the overtones
nor the music one expected
the tones lie
              sibilant.

Twelve Gates to the City

I do not know your entrance
nor would you care for mine
there are many others   but
once we are inside we will meet
and recognize each other
we came our different ways
what a pleasure we are here together.

The Walk Home

There are things which must be said
not always in the words
that saying   merely symbols
for what must be
approximates will not do
begging a question to which
there is no answer
The trade winds from the sea
at turning of the tide
it changes greeting
It is and it is not   A hot day.

Not a Still Life

One petal dropped is
an encapsulated sound
held in what is heard
not muffled   held
so I could hear it
these are the flowers brought inside
how do they sound in falling
out there?

Anger

How do we hear the anger of the birds?
Why are they angry?   (if they are)
There is another anger in the trees
we do not think to hear it
perhaps another kind of it is hidden
in the stones that move below the tides
And some of us burst out as if we knew.

Do not ask for souls
all things possess them
After the stones have turned to sand
there is something other
Leaves in windrows   something other
Do not attempt to define it
in changes   which nothing else may know.

Poor   Old   Tarnished   Flags
they all hang limp
long after their last parades
have vanished   rain and fog
around them   or a breeze that furls
their tired edges
best not to ask why they were hung
such reasons ended in a time
before there were such emblems
Poor   Old   Tired   Flags

A meaning in ‘the silence of pebbles’
is there more than that?   a light
lost to the larger events
at least those thought to be large
there is still that silence
that tells us more
and light to go with it.

Three Beatitudes

Blessed is the man who insisteth not that what has been ignored in favor of a throwaway 'improvement' is obsolete.

Blessed is the man who refuses to settle for an inadequate bandaid to cover a deep wound, physical or political, when a larger means is needed to protect its healing.

Blessed is the man who builds no fences against another's imagined trespass.

Moon Phase

We do not think too often
of the moon's light in the lilacs
too often looking at it   turning
Midas' touch to curse   it's in remembrance
once we see that light   and all around it
blooms   the fading petals in that light
the fading of reflection   light
that was a stranger to the moon
and darkly strange to lilacs as they slept.

Tribute to an Old Family Photograph

She does not respond in any way
that I can tell you   yet she does
to me   if I salute her on my way
upstairs to work at other things
none of which she knows.

Winged Sandal Piece

As if spring colors made things lighter
mirage in fog a   bellbuoy's tone
too soon   too late   this season's trickery
and rocks alive   in spell of it
as if it were   it still might be so
a buoyancy of water as the air's.

Bend's Journey

A

Not straight   the river now against a silence
hard pressed against its own   and so's
the sun or water's bend   a
blending never straightened   pass of either
one to reach   that's for future or the other
not the will of either   in bend those other things
raised out of context   darkening the sun's light
that the water's myriads attempt their places
nor the lack of them   a higher sense   the hulls
the dross of what was water's opening
against a thrust of sun the openings sustain
are fruitful in acceptance   moves and is not
the movement of a hand   what is quiet
is linked to movement   what will come of it
has come   let what it is lie quiet
linked bend to other bend   the move's between
alas for the word   it's a wand caught
in such   the backdraft of waters in a bend
that so they move against each other's flow
as dim-turned water's lave to notch the land
not straight   a straightening to come unheeded

deep water's promise in detritus   banks full chaffed
to wait a falling in another rain let go
to move and carry   as the wand may loose
or bend to pass   no change save silted up
meander done   and there's a bayou
left beyond its river's edge   the mark of it
in marsh and reeds   not straight the sense
of channels once   for companion river's course
thicket in ravine   alluvial as fanned out
impasse   no more to say of it   where once
no clutter where once it was   no course to straighten
that flow of force   that bears away a cruelty
in some regard   but leaves in shards its heritage
that bend's not straight   nor passage to the sea
what'll be of it new weave of what's to come
thought carefully by wand or twist not straightened
without a journey here to there a baring
there   or not so far ashore   no striking point
there is a long   long point to the bend   a longing
some will see it straight as wand reposits movement
trust no measure if the line does nothing
with no curve to measure distance   points as pivots
there is no mattering of distance   how it's reached
the bayou's later   stick to the primal bend
that left the river but made the river's raft
of what encumbered it oblique   still lies
stilling   is the only business of this river's bend
an only river?   or there are the others trying
tributaries to a land of many   from these many lands.

B

Curve of a man not in stature merely shadow
a guess at age only the shadowings are old
light's not there to see the curve mark of doing
what will follow light the fires other light
curved simply as a bend to reach a place for warming
shadow's tricks to spell the age long gone
old curve bend down recourse to river
how does a figure straighten up? let age as spark
take fire from a light on wand to leave it
dark pool of movement wave its wandering
bend not these curves as a man might guess it
stature is/is not the structure of curves as bends
trick of the shadow once again inversion strain
not sadness deepening the length a link say
to old eyes merely see a tilt fooling of a curve
the pool's not straight angles soften into curve
no bend to straighten illusion straightens
curve seen in shadow oh 'stiff diagram of pain'
not straight illusion straightens task a homing
purpose companion to a curve in space no help
an eyeing spent on detail differing is not its reason

as learned   not space alone   a voyage through it
pool of many curves   unnamed though much in seeing
man's curve matters his mark of it   in aging
more distant   disjoint as function poles not primal
see whence and when   eye's revision following
distinct or failing   seen   not for the trust's perception
let go as concept   follows in leitmotif   that music
to straighten becomes a falsehood   cry   and so defined
plunged in false direction up over   black   white   no colors
said to be pedantic   falsifies the text   the straits
for simple passage   never found   curve will hold at bay
there's the trap of logic   door's trap opening
to let the body fall unhoused   its coffin empty
to be used again   not straight   cover's shut
one man at curve was all the bother   not battened
for the bee's trajectory   where does he go from here?
no questions   no lies   performance is another way
failure   with hitches   curves without a thinking
source of intelligence   it will not give to more
bend to the fire   there's the source renewed
blend to the heat's release from borrowed sun
is pivot from/for the curve   bending over it
man's stance   bird bedraggled in the rain
a nourishment to mark the bend   where it disappears
how let these fortunes go?   man and curve his own
enough of spell   a turn for wand   care for eye
will to end it not enough   a pure beginning
wand for heat   or curve   ash drops curving space
within it here as elsewhere   run of river.

C

Straight talk at bend of river   man stood up
from bending   curves to fellow standing   bent to say
voice in blend of rivers   prattle   water's prattling   oh
so very still in bend mind set free as alter task
for talk not stasis   flow from bend   blend   end
from flow to bayou   straits will not do
'where shall we meet   by the river?   not to know
river's bend   curved in the standing   straighten up
authority is useless curve in its way within the bend
as universe is boundless   so the universal
speech unlimited   straits in corsets curved
pay heed to get the news these many convolutions
last of them a straitened   talk   mere gossip
how that suits as will of wind   let be its aiming
that what is common moves against clear river's bend
talk as image of a presence   many present   multifarious
gone many passages   of many traits   hot single   past
reliance   let this river be   curved bend to straighten
long beyond its published strain   what wills centers happening

those many places said to be near shores of Thule
Prester John's   low garble of a sea   beyond such land
'cinch the belt and go on'   past many cinchings said and done
curve of the belt matters where it must   or does not
worn out of play no help   impasse   how to open it
bend of river   movement?   where's the bend of river?
want of passage   how the voice to say it
straight talk won't do   voiced along the many rivers
old man stand up   aligned against the changing curve
how what you meant to say disappears in cinch
straight talk you're blurred   gossip   make the most it
treason's part will follow   bend holds there
long dead   what are words to him?   can't know
without the journey   sounds to follow curve of space
words within themselves at curve   VOICE   above many voices
speech about facts   words about nothing   how they change
clangor about silence   such facts as are voiceless
to be remembered   pure sense of silence voiced over
bend stop curves as curve abounding   particulars let go
density of voices in particulars spent in voyage
let go as hoist up petard   of soundings   some at bend
a darkening of sound wherever   this flow as long as river's
no corners turned   in distances same spot   there have been journeys
curves at many places   multifarious   so said and done
a hovering surprise same spot in movement against own voice
heard at many times the curves let be   spell wand's magic
from each this passing done for presence   sound   wind   hovering
strange source in fickle changes   not of reason opening
the many veins as curves to the heart in cleansing

overheard?   mere logic so attempted   many gists
penstock of reason   reasonings   seen water's flow
offshore gabbling   their types in many waves.

D

Where interim a color   blindness performs as trickster
so modes of major and minor do perform   not black or white
combining all in sadness or joy   of several choices
white or black   combine as blends   or turn to prime
mixed as others   nothing too much   interim left behind
sadness in colors   brown for study   gold as glint
winks out   occasion is not perfect   let it go
bend around river coloring   clotted as froth   flecked cream
interim of color   spectrum's habit   another's depth
bent at blending   verge blue's chill blur red
prime curves instruments of color   coloring to arise
prime to meld   the dark to lighten   wand of purple
as spectrum all that arrives   of a sudden   let be
where interim will follow   what else?   allowance not the trick
black/white   gone beyond   no homesite turned off
to bend   river's courage   course down landing
merely the shuffling of waters   told in many colors
radiance without color does not tell the interim
how to be   space bent   curve of source

color seen   sense before seeing   spectrum's rainbow
curved bend   suppose another   or is it aftermath?
from what is cloud bent   bend of water's coloring
not to trust assumption   water's bend   its coloring
shuffle may (or might)   to blend at bend not straight
straits' narrowing   pinched vase   flows on
strait of blue   straight's red   there is coherence
in not all of it   is what is   the gild and darkening
trajectory one's wand   not gravity alone   of many ways
black/white intrudes   sense bent in color   no truce
known where to bend is color   presumed a knowing
curve straight   only the eye and color   hollah downstream
here's to the drink well watered   course as its portion
old man curved up   belonging to color   hollah again
thread of a way past curve and bend   such colors seemed
let be   of many times the colors   blending over
spell of bend   the later bayous   let be   not joyous
of dun and bright   interim   the rose in petal endures
here's a coming to the clear   at open penstock
sound gabble   something said of journey   wand downstream
more or less in voice of colors   hard to name them
add   in streambank   more's detritus   course   more cannot
some passions cleared   as these   question to the colors
let some be waverings on rainbow's arch   backboned
from many archings   turns to measure   no definition
of many versions impersonal sense   the colors follow
benefit of curve in space   there is no will to it
to wisp of coloring   but others know   are known in following
return   no dread of black or white   the blue's in sense

or red preceding   staff and wand to hold an old man up
above still water's bend   so who's to know it?
long time down spectrum's stream   completing whence.

E

Return is never done on any day   day's ending not complete
sea's bent source turns back through bend   source any day
bend's unlike on such return   likeness not reversed
seen only   eye at bend of color   return   become unlikeness
bend to gabble   no sameness   turned to any tuned motif
at variance may be at crux   a variation not to recognize
or of itself unknown   crook of the bend   its semblance
interim returning   future's bend   clear strait in recognition
of old man's bending over   doubts of return   nor even
turned as no eye to follow   song of a stranger
way faring past meander no lock step to follow fortune's faults
lest it be the quarrying of rock to read that fortune in mishap
notice of beginning   sets the return round each unending
nothing footed   deep morass where once was said to be
there's all of it in sample eye's forewarned   let be to go
future's not to be in light of coloring a shadow
cloud to answer for it   wind to scatter wings imagined
veer off straight imagined curve is not abstraction
idea of straightening a mix in stranglehold not barred

hard part in such imagining   missed in sleight of hand
no future happenstance   something there is not tried or true to form
bend's not made of molds nor to describe itself in surety
turns such belonging to itself   not for new   nor means of it
some things belong to what is elder   some to other reaching
is wonderment   what cannot be fore cast   from cast to cast what is
journeying the past unknown   made by or in what can impede
off course the dreams persist   bend to no likeness
could be where to stop   there is that hazard reached at blow
a stopping at the penstock   held on as such   let go to be
here's willing   glass prosit   all that's old turns anew
before its birth the bend's unlikely   yet   still   coheres
the curve's before us   the new worn old   old man shape changed
known stopping as the river stops   no stop to curve
or bend   cannot scant from blending   what has moved
goes close   the new's not borne   nor old interred
bend is residuum   dependent on such tides of youth
turned elder where the reeds grow into thicket   so impaled
change warrants shape   shape changes   interstices descried
what's sluggish fast in flowing once again and so described
best gaming   such curve bends down   seems straightened
never to the straight once claimed   a simple arrogance
tries distancing   it will not come   nor leasing of the tides
no time   there's shore in recognition   what seems river
to return as marsh   the seas beyond enclosed once more
old man in curve as bend is grieving for the younger
tools left as given   that the young might ask a question
the elder bend no longer present   youth might bend so
reach forgotten curve of river   taken as anew   not so

the secret's not to be less hidden nor explained
gone as for cinch of belt   was fancied lost
return   return is all ways such   a river's loosing   bend!

Astrals

No thing returns/retracts
is nothing   as the words shifting into
them selves create the many
shifts
        we do not bid them
some are re   verberant
some do as some do not
sound in resounding   as
no thing returning nothing
as a leaf   a thing   counts
counts only as no thing
falls to nothing   is retracted
thing in return for nothing
naught might or would be what to fall
as the leaf falls   has fallen more than
nothing   might   weight of wing bent
not a leaf   no leaf at all no
thing as compressed.

Saga   as its saying in the wind   late wind
later than the fall of no thing tuned   nothing
or the catch   once caught in private
a private affair found out: "What are you doing?"
"Nothing.   No thing at all."   No leaf
no sensing   a wind's sensing what was private
saga of no moment   what to say

no thing   no leaf nothing goes to catch a page
not to sense a time cut off from timing
that's a reason in such stellar brilliance
no thing returned/ retracted   nothing
doing no thing   nothing   stellar
actual as the stones.

Goodbye to all that world
where we once talked
as if there were no end
to it   yet went on further
to fall off   even from a globe
held sure by gravity
It is here and not here
a way to walk and say goodbye.

To Be Perennial

Into the eye of the flower
look!
there is another eye looks back
the maiden's eye is shadowed
by a passing bee
but look to the center of that eye
no 'bee loud glade'
from one and then another
into no purpose beyond
the looking
                    fades
can look no more   is heavy
with its fruit and seed.

A Window

1.

A blaze of light surprising winter
only through the panes of glass
protecting it from darkness.

2.

Fickle   not a fault in youth
until it fosters dependence in old age.

3.

Sadness?
too stiff and painful
open the window
the air is sad
as all the wind around it
is not   becoming fresh.

4.

Back to the wind's eye then
shot and focus for the archer
his protection
                        but
a window lets in light.

5.

An end? no ends
fickle as the window is
or
        how it darkens
light?
            be damned
It no longer enters
as we think it did.

Lightning Source UK Ltd.
Milton Keynes UK
UKOW05f0114240617
303961UK00001B/33/P

9 781848 615557